PIERROT
I thought it rather nice.
Well, let us drink some wine and lose our heads
And love each other.

COLUMBINE
Pierrot, don't you love
Me now?

PIERROT
La, what a woman!—how should I know?
Pour me some wine: I'll tell you presently.

COLUMBINE
Pierrot, do you know, I think you drink too much.

PIERROT
Yes, I dare say I do. . . . Or else too little.
It's hard to tell. You see, I am always wanting
A little more than what I have,—or else
A little less. There's something wrong. My dear,
How many fingers have you?

COLUMBINE
La, indeed,
How should I know?—It always takes me one hand
To count the other with. It's too confusing.
Why?

PIERROT
Why?—I am a student, Columbine;
And search into all matters.

COLUMBINE
La, indeed?—
Count them yourself, then!

PIERROT
No. Or, rather, nay.
'Tis of no consequence. . . . I am become
A painter, suddenly,—and you impress me—
Ah, yes!—six orange bull's-eyes, four green pin-wheels,
And one magenta jelly-roll,—the title
As follows: Woman Taking in Cheese from Fire-Escape.

COLUMBINE
Well, I like that! So that is all I've meant

To you!

PIERROT
Hush! All at once I am become
A pianist. I will image you in sound. . . .
On a new scale. . . , Without tonality. . .
Vivace senza tempo senza tutto. . . .
Title: Uptown Express at Six O'Clock.
Pour me a drink.

COLUMBINE
Pierrot, you work too hard.
You need a rest. Come on out into the garden,
And sing me something sad.

PIERROT
Don't stand so near me!
I am become a socialist. I love
Humanity; but I hate people. Columbine,
Put on your mittens, child; your hands are cold.

COLUMBINE
My hands are not cold!

PIERROT
Oh, I am sure they are.
And you must have a shawl to wrap about you,
And sit by the fire.

COLUMBINE
Why, I'll do no such thing!
I'm hot as a spoon in a teacup!

PIERROT
Columbine,
I'm a philanthropist. I know I am,
Because I feel so restless. Do not scream,
Or it will be the worse for you!

COLUMBINE
Pierrot,
My vinaigrette! I cannot live without
My vinaigrette!

PIERROT
My only love, you are
So fundamental! . . . How would you like to be
An actress, Columbine?—I am become

Aria da Capo by Edna St Vincent Millay

Edna St. Vincent Millay was born on 22nd February 1892 in Rockland, Maine, the eldest of three daughters.

Her early years were tinted with much difficulty; divorced parents, poverty and a constant change of location.

Despite this once settled in Camden, Maine Edna developed her literary talents at a furious rate. By 15, she had published her poetry in the popular children's magazine St. Nicholas, the Camden Herald, and the high-profile anthology Current Literature.

In 1912, at 20, she entered her poem 'Renascence' in The Lyric Year poetry contest. Despite being considered the best poem it was only given fourth place. The ensuing uproar brought publicity and the offer of funding for her education at Vassar College. Here she wrote, both verse and plays as well as embarking on a series of affairs with women as she explored the wider world and all it offered.

Edna achieved significant fame when she won the Pulitzer Prize for Poetry in 1923 for 'The Ballad of the Harp-Weaver'. It was a magnificent triumph.

She married Eugen Jan Boissevain but on her wedding day she fell ill and he drove her to Manhattan for emergency surgery. He nursed her back to health with remarkable devotion. They were together, in an open marriage, until his death in 1949.

In the summer of 1936, Edna was riding in a station wagon when the door swung open and she was hurled into the pitch-darkness and rolled into a rocky gully. She survived but with severely damaged nerves in her spine and was to live the rest of her life in pain.

In 1942 in an article for The New York Times Magazine, Edna mourned the callous destruction of the Czechoslovak town of Lidice by Nazi forces in retaliation for the assassination of Reinhard Heydrich. The article would serve as the basis of her 32-page poem, 'Murder of Lidice' in 1942.

Edna St. Vincent Millay, after suffering a heart attack, fell down the stairs and died at her home on 19th October 1950. She was 58 years old.

Index of Contents
PERSONS
SCENE: A stage
ARIA DA CAPO
AUTHOR'S NOTE ON THE PLAYING OF ARIA DA CAPO
ORIGINAL CAST
AUTHOR'S NOTE
SUGGESTIONS FOR THE PRODUCTION OF "ARIA DA CAPO"
SETTING
PROPERTIES

COSTUMES
CHARACTERS
EDNA ST VINCENT MILLAY – A SHORT BIOGRAPHY
EDNA ST VINCENT MILLAY – A CONCISE BIBLIOGRAPHY

PERSONS
Pierrot
Columbine
Cothurnus, Masque of Tragedy
Thyrsis, Shepherd
Corydon, Shepherds

SCENE: A stage

ARIA DA CAPO

[The curtain rises on a stage set for a Harlequinade, a merry black and white interior. Directly behind the footlights, and running parallel with them, is a long table, covered with a gay black and white cloth, on which is spread a banquet. At the opposite ends of this table, seated on delicate thin-legged chairs with high backs, are **PIERROT** and **COLUMBINE**, dressed according to the tradition, excepting that **PIERROT** is in lilac, and **COLUMBINE** in pink. They are dining.

COLUMBINE
Pierrot, a macaroon! I cannot live without a macaroon!

PIERROT
My only love,
You are so intense! . . . Is it Tuesday, Columbine?—
I'll kiss you if it's Tuesday.

COLUMBINE
It is Wednesday,
If you must know . . . . Is this my artichoke,
Or yours?

PIERROT
Ah, Columbine,—as if it mattered!
Wednesday . . . . Will it be Tuesday, then, to-morrow,
By any chance?

COLUMBINE
To-morrow will be—Pierrot,
That isn't funny!

Your manager.

COLUMBINE
Why, Pierrot, I can't act.

PIERROT
Can't act! Can't act! La, listen to the woman!
What's that to do with the price of furs?—You're blonde,
Are you not?—you have no education, have you?—
Can't act! You underrate yourself, my dear!

COLUMBINE
Yes, I suppose I do.

PIERROT
As for the rest,
I'll teach you how to cry, and how to die,
And other little tricks; and the house will love you.
You'll be a star by five o'clock . . . that is,
If you will let me pay for your apartment.

COLUMBINE
Let you?—well, that's a good one!
Ha! Ha! Ha!
But why?

PIERROT
But why?—well, as to that, my dear,
I cannot say. It's just a matter of form.

COLUMBINE
Pierrot, I'm getting tired of caviar
And peacocks' livers. Isn't there something else
That people eat?—some humble vegetable,
That grows in the ground?

PIERROT
Well, there are mushrooms.

COLUMBINE
Mushrooms!
That's so! I had forgotten . . . mushrooms . . . mushrooms. . . .
I cannot live with . . . How do you like this gown?

PIERROT
Not much. I'm tired of gowns that have the waist-line
About the waist, and the hem around the bottom,—
And women with their breasts in front of them!—

Zut and ehè! Where does one go from here!

COLUMBINE
Here's a persimmon, love. You always liked them.

PIERROT
I am become a critic; there is nothing
I can enjoy. . . . However, set it aside;
I'll eat it between meals.

COLUMBINE
Pierrot, do you know,
Sometimes I think you're making fun of me.

PIERROT
My love, by yon black moon, you wrong us both.

COLUMBINE
There isn't a sign of a moon, Pierrot.

PIERROT
Of course not.
There never was. "Moon's" just a word to swear by.
"Mutton!"—now there's a thing you can lay the hands on,
And set the tooth in! Listen, Columbine:
I always lied about the moon and you.
Food is my only lust.

COLUMBINE
Well, eat it, then,
For Heaven's sake, and stop your silly noise!
I haven't heard the clock tick for an hour.

PIERROT
It's ticking all the same. If you were a fly,
You would be dead by now. And if I were a parrot,
I could be talking for a thousand years!

[Enter **COTHURNUS**.

PIERROT
Hello, what's this, for God's sake?—
What's the matter?
Say, whadda you mean?—get off the stage, my friend,
And pinch yourself,—you're walking in your sleep!

COTHURNUS
I never sleep.

PIERROT
Well, anyhow, clear out.
You don't belong on here. Wait for your own scene!
Whadda you think this is,—a dress-rehearsal?

COTHURNUS
Sir, I am tired of waiting. I will wait
No longer.

PIERROT
Well, but whadda you going to do?
The scene is set for me!

COTHURNUS
True, sir; yet I
Can play the scene.

PIERROT
Your scene is down for later!

COTHURNUS
That, too, is true, sir; but I play it now.

PIERROT
Oh, very well!—Anyway, I am tired
Of black and white. At least, I think I am.

[Exit **COLUMBINE**.

Yes, I am sure I am. I know what I'll do!—
I'll go and strum the moon, that's what I'll do. . . .
Unless, perhaps . . . you never can tell . . . I may be,
You know, tired of the moon. Well, anyway,
I'll go find Columbine. . . . And when I find her,
I will address her thus: "Ehè, Pierrette!"—
There's something in that.

[Exit **PIERROT**.

COTHURNUS
You, Thyrsis! Corydon!
Where are you?

THYRSIS [Off stage]
Sir, we are in our dressing-room!

COTHURNUS

Come out and do the scene.

CORYDON [Off stage]
You are mocking us!—
The scene is down for later.

COTHURNUS
That is true;
But we will play it now. I am the scene.

[Seats himself on high place in back of stage.

[Enter **CORYDON** and **THYRSIS**.

CORYDON
Sir, we are counting on this little hour.
We said, "Here is an hour,—in which to think
A mighty thought, and sing a trifling song,
And look at nothing."—And, behold! the hour,
Even as we spoke, was over, and the act begun,
Under our feet!

THYRSIS
Sir, we are not in the fancy
To play the play. We had thought to play it later.

CORYDON
Besides, this is the setting for a farce.
Our scene requires a wall; we cannot build
A wall of tissue-paper!

THYRSIS
We cannot act
A tragedy with comic properties!

COTHURNUS
Try it and see. I think you'll find you can.
One wall is like another. And regarding
The matter of your insufficient mood,
The important thing is that you speak the lines,
And make the gestures. Wherefore I shall remain
Throughout, and hold the prompt-book. Are you ready?

CORYDON-THYRSIS [Sorrowfully]
Sir, we are always ready.

COTHURNUS
Play the play!

[**CORYDON** and **THYRSIS** move the table and chairs to one side out of the way, and seat themselves in a half-reclining position on the floor.

THYRSIS
How gently in the silence, Corydon,
Our sheep go up the bank. They crop a grass
That's yellow where the sun is out, and black
Where the clouds drag their shadows. Have you noticed
How steadily, yet with what a slanting eye
They graze?

CORYDON
As if they thought of other things.
What say you, Thyrsis, do they only question
Where next to pull?—Or do their far minds draw them
Thus vaguely north of west and south of east?

THYRSIS
One cannot say. . . . The black lamb wears its burdocks
As if they were a garland,—have you noticed?
Purple and white—and drinks the bitten grass
As if it were a wine.

CORYDON
I've noticed that.
What say you, Thyrsis, shall we make a song
About a lamb that thought himself a shepherd?

THYRSIS
Why, yes!—that is, why,—no. (I have forgotten my line.)

COTHURNUS [Prompting]
"I know a game worth two of that!"

THYRSIS
Oh, yes. . . . I know a game worth two of that!
Let's gather rocks, and build a wall between us;
And say that over there belongs to me,
And over here to you!

CORYDON
Why,—very well.
And say you may not come upon my side
Unless I say you may!

THYRSIS
Nor you on mine!

And if you should, 'twould be the worse for you!

[They weave a wall of colored crêpe paper ribbons from the centre front to the centre back of the stage, fastening the ends to **COLUMBINE'S** chair in front and to **PIERROT'S** chair in the back.

CORYDON
Now there's a wall a man may see across,
But not attempt to scale.

THYRSIS
An excellent wall.

CORYDON
Come, let us separate, and sit alone
A little while, and lay a plot whereby
We may outdo each other.

[They seat themselves on opposite sides of the wall.

PIERROT [Off stage]
Ehè, Pierrette!

COLUMBINE [Off stage]
My name is Columbine!
Leave me alone!

THYRSIS [Coming up to the wall]
Corydon, after all, and in spite of the fact
I started it myself, I do not like this
So very much. What is the sense of saying
I do not want you on my side the wall?
It is a silly game. I'd much prefer
Making the little song you spoke of making,
About the lamb, you know, that thought himself
A shepherd!—what do you say?

[Pause.

CORYDON [At wall]
(I have forgotten the line.)

COTHURNUS [Prompting]
"How do I know this isn't a trick?"

CORYDON
Oh, yes. . . . How do I know this isn't a trick
To get upon my land?

THYRSIS
Oh, Corydon,
You know it's not a trick. I do not like
The game, that's all. Come over here, or let me
Come over there.

CORYDON
It is a clever trick
To get upon my land.

[Seats himself as before.

THYRSIS
Oh, very well!
[Seats himself as before]
[To himself]
I think I never knew a sillier game.

CORYDON [Coming to wall]
Oh, Thyrsis, just a minute!—all the water
Is on your side the wall, and the sheep are thirsty.
I hadn't thought of that.

THYRSIS
Oh, hadn't you?

CORYDON
Why, what do you mean?

THYRSIS
What do I mean?—I mean
That I can play a game as well as you can.
And if the pool is on my side, it's on
My side, that's all.

CORYDON
You mean you'd let the sheep
Go thirsty?

THYRSIS
Well, they're not my sheep. My sheep
Have water enough.

CORYDON
Your sheep! You are mad, to call them
Yours—mine—they are all one flock! Thyrsis, you can't mean
To keep the water from them, just because
They happened to be grazing over here

Instead of over there, when we set the wall up?

THYRSIS
Oh, can't I?—wait and see!—and if you try
To lead them over here, you'll wish you hadn't!

CORYDON
I wonder how it happens all the water
Is on your side. . . . I'll say you had an eye out
For lots of little things, my innocent friend,
When I said, "Let us make a song," and you said,
"I know a game worth two of that!"

COLUMBINE [Off stage]
Pierrot,
D'you know, I think you must be getting old,
Or fat, or something,—stupid, anyway!—
Can't you put on some other kind of collar?

THYRSIS
You know as well as I do, Corydon,
I never thought anything of the kind.
Don't you?

CORYDON
I do not.

THYRSIS
Don't you?

CORYDON
Oh, I suppose so.
Thyrsis, let's drop this,—what do you say?—it's only
A game, you know . . . we seem to be forgetting
It's only a game ... a pretty serious game
It's getting to be, when one of us is willing
To let the sheep go thirsty for the sake of it.

THYRSIS
I know it, Corydon.

[They reach out their arms to each other across the wall.]

COTHURNUS [Prompting]
"But how do I know—"

THYRSIS
Oh, yes. . . . But how do I know this isn't a trick

To water your sheep, and get the laugh on me?

CORYDON
You can't know, that's the difficult thing about it,
Of course,—you can't be sure. You have to take
My word for it. And I know just how you feel.
But one of us has to take a risk, or else,
Why, don't you see?—the game goes on forever! . . .
It's terrible, when you stop to think of it. . . .
Oh, Thyrsis, now for the first time I feel
This wall is actually a wall, a thing
Come up between us, shutting you away
From me. . . . I do not know you any more!

THYRSIS
No, don't say that! Oh, Corydon, I'm willing
To drop it all, if you will! Come on over
And water your sheep! It is an ugly game.
I hated it from the first. . . . How did it start?

CORYDON
I do not know . . . I do not know . . . I think
I am afraid of you!—you are a stranger!
I never set eyes on you before! "Come over
And water my sheep," indeed!—They'll be more thirsty
Than they are now before I bring them over
Into your land, and have you mixing them up
With yours, and calling them yours, and trying to keep them!

[Enter **COLUMBINE**.

COLUMBINE [To **COTHURNUS**]
Glummy, I want my hat.

THYRSIS
Take it, and go.

COLUMBINE
Take it and go, indeed. Is it my hat,
Or isn't it? Is this my scene, or not?
Take it and go! Really, you know, you two
Are awfully funny!

[Exit **COLUMBINE**.

THYRSIS
Corydon, my friend,
I'm going to leave you now, and whittle me

A pipe, or sing a song, or go to sleep.
When you have come to your senses, let me know.

[Goes back to where he has been sitting, lies down and sleeps.

[**CORYDON**, in going back to where he has been sitting, stumbles over bowl of colored confetti and colored paper ribbons.

CORYDON
Why, what is this?—Red stones—and purple stones—
And stones stuck full of gold!—The ground is full
Of gold and colored stones! . . . I'm glad the wall
Was up before I found them!—Otherwise,
I should have had to share them. As it is,
They all belong to me. . . . Unless—

[He goes to wall and digs up and down the length of it, to see if there are jewels on the other side.

None here—
None here—none here—They all belong to me!

[Sits.

THYRSIS [Awakening]
How curious! I thought the little black lamb
Came up and licked my hair; I saw the wool
About its neck as plain as anything!
It must have been a dream. The little black lamb
Is on the other side of the wall, I'm sure.

[Goes to wall and looks over. **CORYDON** is seated on the ground, tossing the confetti up into the air and catching it.

Hello, what's that you've got there, Corydon?

CORYDON
Jewels.

THYRSIS
Jewels?—And where did you ever get them?

CORYDON
Oh, over here.

THYRSIS
You mean to say you found them,
By digging around in the ground for them?

CORYDON [Unpleasantly]
No, Thyrsis,
By digging down for water for my sheep.

THYRSIS
Corydon, come to the wall a minute, will you?
I want to talk to you.

CORYDON
I haven't time.
I'm making me a necklace of red stones.

THYRSIS
I'll give you all the water that you want,
For one of those red stones,—if it's a good one.

CORYDON
Water?—what for?—what do I want of water?

THYRSIS
Why, for your sheep!

CORYDON
My sheep?—I'm not a shepherd!

THYRSIS
Your sheep are dying of thirst.

CORYDON
Man, haven't I told you
I can't be bothered with a few untidy
Brown sheep all full of burdocks?—I'm a merchant.
That's what I am!—And if I set my mind to it
I dare say I could be an emperor!
[To himself]
Wouldn't I be a fool to spend my time
Watching a flock of sheep go up a hill,
When I have these to play with?—when I have these
To think about?—I can't make up my mind
Whether to buy a city, and have a thousand
Beautiful girls to bathe me, and be happy
Until I die, or build a bridge, and name it
The Bridge of Corydon,—and be remembered
After I'm dead.

THYRSIS
Corydon, come to the wall,
Won't you?—I want to tell you something.

CORYDON
Hush!
Be off! Be off! Go finish your nap, I tell you!

THYRSIS
Corydon, listen: if you don't want your sheep,
Give them to me.

CORYDON
Be off! Go finish your nap.
A red one—and a blue one—and a red one—
And a purple one—give you my sheep, did you say?—
Come, come! What do you take me for, a fool?
I've a lot of thinking to do,—and while I'm thinking,
The sheep might just as well be over here
As over there. . . . A blue one—and a red one—

THYRSIS
But they will die!

CORYDON
And a green one—and a couple
Of white ones, for a change.

THYRSIS
Maybe I have
Some jewels on my side.

CORYDON
And another green one—
Maybe, but I don't think so. You see, this rock
Isn't so very wide. It stops before
It gets to the wall. It seems to go quite deep,
However.

THYRSIS [With hatred]
I see.

COLUMBINE [Off stage]
Look, Pierrot, there's the moon.

PIERROT [Off stage]
Nonsense!

THYRSIS
I see.

COLUMBINE [Off stage]
Sing me an old song, Pierrot,—
Something I can remember.

PIERROT [Off stage]
Columbine.
Your mind is made of crumbs,—like an escallop
Of oysters,—first a layer of crumbs, and then
An oystery taste, and then a layer of crumbs.

THYRSIS [Searching]
I find no jewels . . . but I wonder what
The root of this black weed would do to a man
If he should taste it. ... I have seen a sheep die,
With half the stalk still drooling from its mouth.
'Twould be a speedy remedy, I should think,
For a festered pride and a feverish ambition.
It has a curious root. I think I'll hack it
In little pieces. . . . First I'll get me a drink;
And then I'll hack that root in little pieces
As small as dust, and see what the color is
Inside.

[Goes to bowl on floor.

The pool is very clear. I see
A shepherd standing on the brink, with a red cloak
About him, and a black weed in his hand. . . .
'Tis I.

[Kneels and drinks.

CORYDON [Coming to wall]
Hello, what are you doing, Thyrsis?

THYRSIS
Digging for gold.

CORYDON
I'll give you all the gold
You want, if you'll give me a bowl of water.
If you don't want too much, that is to say.

THYRSIS
Ho, so you've changed your mind?—It's different,
Isn't it, when you want a drink yourself?

CORYDON

Of course it is.

THYRSIS
Well, let me see ... a bowl
Of water,—come back in an hour, Corydon.
I'm busy now.

CORYDON
Oh, Thyrsis, give me a bowl
Of water!—and I'll fill the bowl with jewels,
And bring it back!

THYRSIS
Be off, I'm busy now.

[He catches sight of the weed, picks it up and looks at it, unseen by **CORYDON**.

Wait!—Pick me out the finest stones you have . . .
I'll bring you a drink of water presently.

CORYDON [Goes back and sits down, with the jewels before him]
A bowl of jewels is a lot of jewels.

THYRSIS [Chopping up the weed]
I wonder if it has a bitter taste.

CORYDON
There's sure to be a stone or two among them
I have grown fond of, pouring them from one hand
Into the other.

THYRSIS
I hope it doesn't taste
Too bitter, just at first.

CORYDON
A bowl of jewels
Is far too many jewels to give away
And not get back again.

THYRSIS
I don't believe
He'll notice. He's too thirsty. He'll gulp it down
And never notice.

CORYDON
There ought to be some way
To get them back again. . . . I could give him a necklace,

And snatch it back, after I'd drunk the water,
I suppose. . . . Why, as for that, of course a necklace. . . .

[He puts two or three of the colored tapes together and tries their strength by pulling them, after which he puts them around his neck and pulls them, gently, nodding to himself. He gets up and goes to the wall, with the colored tapes in his hands.

[THYRSIS in the meantime has poured the powdered root—black confetti—into the pot which contained the flower and filled it up with wine from the punch-bowl on the floor. He comes to the wall at the same time, holding the bowl of poison.

THYRSIS
Come, get your bowl of water, Corydon.

CORYDON
Ah, very good!—and for such a gift as that
I'll give you more than a bowl of unset stones.
I'll give you three long necklaces, my friend.
Come closer. Here they are.

[Puts the ribbons about **THYRSIS'** neck.

THYRSIS [Putting bowl to **CORYDON'S** mouth]
I'll hold the bowl
Until you've drunk it all.

CORYDON
Then hold it steady.
For every drop you spill I'll have a stone back
Out of this chain.

THYRSIS
I shall not spill a drop.

[**CORYDON** drinks, meanwhile beginning to strangle **THYRSIS**.

THYRSIS
Don't pull the string so tight.

CORYDON
You're spilling the water.

THYRSIS
You've had enough—you've had enough—stop pulling
The string so tight!

CORYDON
Why, that's not tight at all ...

How's this?

THYRSIS [Drops bowl]
You're strangling me! Oh, Corydon!
It's only a game!—and you are strangling me!

CORYDON: It's only a game, is it?—Yet I believe
You've poisoned me in earnest!

[Writhes and pulls the strings tighter, winding them about **THYRSIS'** neck.

THYRSIS
Corydon!

[Dies.

CORYDON
You've poisoned me in earnest. . . . I feel so cold. . . .
So cold . . . this is a very silly game. . . .
Why do we play it?—let's not play this game
A minute more . . . let's make a little song
About a lamb. . . . I'm coming over the wall,
No matter what you say,—I want to be near you. . . .

[Groping his way, with arms wide before him, he strides through the frail papers of the wall without knowing it, and continues seeking for the wall straight across the stage.

Where is the wall?

[Gropes his way back, and stands very near **THYRSIS** without seeing him; he speaks slowly.

There isn't any wall,
I think.

[Takes a step forward, his foot touches **THYRSIS'** body, and he falls down beside him.

Thyrsis, where is your cloak?—just give me
A little bit of your cloak! . . .

[Draws corner of **THYRSIS'** cloak over his shoulders, falls across **THYRSIS'** body, and dies.

[**COTHURNUS** closes the prompt-book with a bang, arises matter-of-factly, comes down stage, and places the table over the two bodies, drawing down the cover so that they are hidden from any actors on the stage, but visible to the audience, pushing in their feet and hands with his boot. He then turns his back to the audience, and claps his hands twice.

COTHURNUS
Strike the scene!

[Exit **COTHURNUS**.

[Enter **PIERROT** and **COLUMBINE**.

PIERROT
Don't puff so, Columbine!

COLUMBINE
Lord, what a mess
This set is in! If there's one thing I hate
Above everything else,—even more than getting my feet wet—
It's clutter!—He might at least have left the scene
The way he found it ... don't you say so, Pierrot?

[She picks up punch bowl. They arrange chairs as before at ends of table.

PIERROT
Well, I don't know. I think it rather diverting
The way it is.

[Yawns, picks up confetti bowl.

Shall we begin?

COLUMBINE [Screams]
My God!
What's that there under the table?

PIERROT
It is the bodies
Of the two shepherds from the other play.

COLUMBINE [Slowly]
How curious to strangle him like that,
With colored paper ribbons.

PIERROT
Yes, and yet
I dare say he is just as dead.
[Pauses. Calls]
Cothurnus!
Come drag these bodies out of here! We can't
Sit down and eat with two dead bodies lying
Under the table! . . . The audience wouldn't stand for it!

COTHURNUS [Off stage]
What makes you think so?—

Pull down the tablecloth
On the other side, and hide them from the house,
And play the farce. The audience will forget.

PIERROT
That's so. Give me a hand there,
Columbine.

[**PIERROT** and **COLUMBINE** pull down the table cover in such a way that the two bodies are hidden from the house, then merrily set their bowls back on the table, draw up their chairs, and begin the play exactly as before.

COLUMBINE
Pierrot, a macaroon,—I cannot live without a macaroon!

PIERROT
My only love,
You are so intense! ... Is it Tuesday, Columbine?—
I'll kiss you if it's Tuesday.

[Curtains begin to close slowly.

COLUMBINE
It is Wednesday,
If you must know. ... Is this my artichoke
Or yours?

PIERROT
Ah, Columbine, as if it mattered!
Wednesday. . . . Will it be Tuesday, then, to-morrow,
By any chance? . . .

[CURTAIN.

AUTHOR'S NOTE ON THE PLAYING OF ARIA DA CAPO

ORIGINAL CAST

AS PLAYED BY THE PROVINCETOWN PLAYERS, NEW YORK CITY

PIERROT	HARRISON DOWD
COLUMBINE	NORMA MILLAY
COTHURNUS	HUGH FERRISS
CORYDON	CHARLES ELLIS
THYRSIS	JAMES LIGHT

So great is my vexation always, when reading a play, to find its progress constantly being halted and its structure loosened by elaborate explanatory parentheses, that I resolved when I should publish Aria da Capo to incorporate into its text only those explanations the omission of which might confuse the reader or lend a wrong interpretation to the lines. Since, however, Aria da Capo was written not only to be read but also to be acted, and being conscious that the exclusion of the usual directions, while clarifying the play to the reader, may make it bare of suggestions and somewhat baffling to the producer, I am adding here some remarks which have been found of value in preparing it for presentation on the stage.

Since the production of Aria da Capo by the Provincetown Players, I have received a great many letters from the directors of little theatres, asking for copies of it with a view to producing it. Very often, after I send the play, I receive a letter in reply asking for some suggestions for its presentation, and enclosing direct questions on points that have been difficult. It occurred to me finally that it would be reasonable to make up a sort of informal prompt-book to send about with the play; and it is that which is printed below. It will be found incomplete and uneven, in some instances unnecessarily detailed, in others not sufficiently so; all of which is due to the fact that it was put together loosely, from answers to chance questions, rather than logically, as an entity in itself.

SUGGESTIONS FOR THE PRODUCTION OF "ARIA DA CAPO"

SETTING:

The setting required is simple:—a grey curtain, a long black table, two slender black high-backed chairs, and a raised platform.

Instead of wings and back-drop the Provincetown Players cleverly utilized painted screens, the heights varying from 6 to 10 feet, these being set right and left of the stage in such manner as to give the effect of depth and distance.

The table, six feet long and two feet wide, has thin legs and is painted black.

When Pierrot and Columbine enter in the final scene, it is not necessary that the table which Cothurnus has replaced shall entirely conceal the bodies of Thyrsis and Corydon. Pierrot and Columbine must ignore them until the lines indicate their discovery, no matter how they may have fallen.

Particular attention must be given to the chairs in this set. They are used to construct the tissue-paper wall, and, although delicate, should be heavy enough to remain solid and steady, up and down stage, without the possibility of an upset when Corydon strides through the wall.

Near the footlights (actors' left) are two sofa pillows, used to represent the rocks against which the shepherds lean. On the left of the stage have another pillow, which Thyrsis places under his head when he lies down to sleep. Use cloth or crêpe paper for these pillows, and have them of spotted black and white material, or of any gay color except red or blue.

Cothurnus occupies a chair upon a platform, up-stage, centre, with two or three steps surrounding it on three sides. Drape this with plain heavy black cloth.

The table covering is important. Its width is equal to that of the added height and width of the table. As it must be moved to cover the bodies of Thyrsis and Corydon, it should be of sufficient weight to prevent slipping. It will be well to experiment with this, to ensure proper performance.

The cover should have black and white spots and striped ends.

The table is set as follows:—two large wooden bowls (at least seven inches high and fourteen inches in diameter). One is placed at each end of the table. That at Columbine's end should contain persimmons, pomegranates, grapes and other bright exotic fruits. Pierrot's bowl has confetti and colored paper ribbons, the latter showing plainly over the edge. (If Columbine uses practical macaroons, put them into this bowl.)

Near Columbine, place a practical uncooked artichoke; have this of good size, and nail it to a wooden standard, painted black. At both places there are tall white wooden goblets.

In the centre of the table there should be a curious, grotesque, but very gay flower, standing upright in a pot of wood or heavy paper, which will not break when Thyrsis drops it. Concealed at the root of this plant there should be a small sack of black confetti, to be used in the "poison scene."

The table should be set with nothing but these articles, and yet give the appearance of bounty and elegance.

Place the table parallel with the footlights,—the long side toward the audience.

Columbine's chair is at the actors' right, and Pierrot's opposite—Columbine's hat hangs from her chair-top. Both chairs are festooned with tissue-paper ribbons, at least ten feet long, to be used later by the shepherds to represent their wall. These must be of such a texture as to break readily when Corydon walks through, and a prearranged transverse tear or two will assist in the prompt breakage when he does so.

PROPERTIES:

Two white wooden bowls, one filled with fruits and the other with confetti and paper ribbons,—one ribbon to be of cotton or silk, in order to be not too easily broken by Corydon when strangling Thyrsis

Two tall white wooden goblets

One artichoke nailed to a standard

One flower in paper or wooden pot, the root wrapped with black crêpe paper (or use confetti)

Black and white tablecloth

Macaroons

Boots and prompt-book for Cothurnus (large flat black book)

Also, if desired, mask of Tragedy for Cothurnus

Crêpe or tissue streamers of different colors, including no red or blue, for wall.

COSTUMES:

PIERROT
Lavender or lilac satin, preferably a blue-lavender. Care should be taken that the lavender does not turn pink under the stage lights. Pierrot's costume is the conventional smock with wide trousers, with black crêpe paper rosettes on the smock, wide white tarleton ruff. Black evening pumps with black rosettes may be worn. Black silk skull-cap.

COLUMBINE
Tight black satin bodice cut very low, with straps over the shoulders, quite like the modern evening gown; very full tarleton skirts of different shades of pink and cerise, reaching to the knees; ruffled bloomers of apple-green tarleton, the ruffles showing below the skirts; black silk stockings and black ballet slippers, laced with green. Hat of lavender crêpe paper, with streamers of gay colors—including, however, no clear red or blue. Hat should be small and very smart—not a shepherdess hat. Columbine should be made up to suggest a doll. As originally interpreted she had short light hair, standing out bushily all over her head. Long hair should be rolled under to give a bobbed effect, or could be arranged in obvious caricature of some extreme modern style, but must look attractive, and must be blonde.

COTHURNUS
Plain toga of dull purple in some heavy, unreflecting material which will fall into large folds, lined with sombre flame-color; a garment with large purple sleeves, of which only the sleeves were visible, was worn under the toga,—but the effect should be classical; heavy boots should be worn, as nearly as possible like the tragic Roman buskin; one end of the great toga is tied into a rough hood which covers the actor's head; a mask may be worn, but it is often difficult to speak through, and, if desired, the actor's face may be made up to represent a mask of Tragedy.

THYRSIS and CORYDON
These costumes, in striking contrast to the elegance of those of Pierrot and Columbine, should be very simple, and very roughly made; short tunics of outing-flannel or some such material—fastened loosely over one shoulder,—one shoulder, as well as most of the back and breast, exposed. Legs bare, or swathed from the knee to the ankle in rough strips of the same material. Sandals. Cloaks of heavier, cheap material fastened to the tunics in such a way that they will appear to be simply flung over the shoulder, but actually fastened very cleverly in order to avoid tripping the shepherds, who are continually sitting down on the floor and getting up again.

Thyrsis wears a dark grey tunic and cloak of raw bright red,—but not a turkey-red, as this color will kill the blue of Corydon's cloak. Corydon wears tunic of light grey and cloak of brilliant blue. There must be no red or blue used anywhere in the entire play excepting in the blue and red of these two cloaks. The two shepherds must be so strong and vivid in every way that when Columbine comes in and says, "Is this my scene or not?" it will seem to the audience that it is she, not the shepherds, who is hopelessly out of the scene.

CHARACTERS:

PIERROT

Pierrot sees clearly into existing evils and is rendered gaily cynical by them; he is both too indolent and too indifferent to do anything about it. Yet in several lines of the play his actual unhappiness is seen,— for instance, "Moon's just a word to swear by," in which he expresses his conviction that all beauty and romance are fled from the world. At the end of the play the line, "Yes, and yet I dare say he is just as dead," must not be said flippantly or cynically, but slowly and with much philosophic concentration on the thought. From the moment when Columbine cries, "What's that there under the table?" until Pierrot calls, "Cothurnus, come drag these bodies out of here!" they both stand staring at the two bodies, without moving in any way, or even lifting their eyes. (This same holding of the play is used several times also by the shepherds,—for instance, always during the off-stage interpolations, they stand either staring at each other across the wall, or maintaining whatever other position they may have had when the off-stage voice begins speaking, until the interruption is over, when they resume their drama quite as if nobody had spoken.) Columbine's "How curious to strangle him like that" is spoken extremely slowly, in a voice of awe, curiosity, and horror. For a moment the two characters seem almost to feel and be subdued by the tragedy that has taken place. They remain standing very quietly while Cothurnus speaks his final lines off stage, and for a moment after he has said, "The audience will forget"; then very slowly raise their eyes and exchange glances, Pierrot nods his head curtly and says, "That's so"; they set their bowls gaily back on the table, and the play begins again.

Pierrot in such lines as "Ah, Columbine, as if it mattered!" speaks with mock saccharine tenderness; but in such lines as "If you were a fly you would be dead by now!" although he speaks very gaily his malice must be apparent almost even to her; Columbine bores him to death. When he says, "I'll go and strum the moon!" he is for the instant genuinely excited and interested; he is for this moment like a child, and is happy.

COLUMBINE

Pretty and charming, but stupid; she never knows what Pierrot is talking about, and is so accustomed to him that she no longer pretends to understand him; but she is very proud of him, and when he speaks she listens with trustful admiration. Her expression, "I cannot live without" this or that, is a phrase she uses in order to make herself more attractive, because she believes men prefer women to be useless and extravagant; if left to herself she would be a domestic and capable person.

COTHURNUS

This character should be played by a tall and imposing figure with a tremendous voice. The voice of Cothurnus is one of the most important things in the acting play. He should have a voice deeper than the voice used by any of the other persons, should speak weightily and with great dignity, but almost without intonation, and quite without feeling, as if he had said the same words many times before. Only in his last speech may he be permitted a comment on the situation. This speech should be spoken quite as impressively as the others and fully as slowly.

CORYDON and **THYRSIS**

These two characters are young, very simple, and childlike; they are acted upon by the force that sits on the back of the stage behind them. More and more as their quarrel advances they begin to see that something is wrong, but they have no idea what to do about it, and they scarcely realize what is happening, the quarrel grows so from little things into big things. Corydon's first vision of the tragedy is in "It's terrible when you stop to think of it." Thyrsis' first vision comes when he looks into the pool; in seeing the familiar reflection he is struck by the unfamiliarity of one aspect of it, the poisonous root; for the first time he realizes that this man who is about to kill with poisoned water his most beloved friend, is none other than Thyrsis himself,—"'Tis I!" The personalities of Thyrsis and Corydon are not essentially different. They develop somewhat differently, because of the differing circumstances.

When Columbine goes out for the first time she takes with her her artichoke and her wine-glass, also a couple of macaroons, which she nibbles, going out. This helps to get the table cleared. The other articles are removed by the shepherds when they prepare the stage for their scene, in this manner: at the cue "Sir, we are always ready. . . . Play the play!", Corydon and Thyrsis come down stage, Corydon to Pierrot's end of the table, Thyrsis to Columbia's; simultaneously, first, they set back the chairs against the wall, Pierrot's left front, Columbine's right front; next they remove the two big bowls and set them in symmetrical positions on the floor, left front and right front, in such a way that the bowl of confetti may be the mine of jewels for Corydon, and the bowl of fruits, the punch-bowl, may represent the pool of water for Thyrsis; then, taking the table by the two ends, they set it back against the wall, right; next, while Corydon places the two pillows from the left wall on the floor to represent rocks in their pasture, Thyrsis removes from the table everything that is left on it except the tablecloth,—this should be only Pierrot's wine-goblet and the flower in its pot. (The flower is to represent later the poisonous weed which Thyrsis finds, the wine-goblet a drinking-cup beside the pool, the flower-pot a bowl in which to mix the poison and bring it to Corydon.) The two shepherds do this setting of their stage swiftly and silently, then seat themselves at once, in easy but beautiful postures, and remain for a moment looking off as if at their sheep while a complete silence settles over the stage and house,—a pastoral silence, if it is possible to suggest it—before they begin to speak.

When Columbine comes in, looking for her hat, she picks up the hat from her chair, now in the centre of the stage near the footlights, in a direct line with Pierrot's, which is centre back, just in front of Cothurnus,—the shepherds having set them in these positions, back to back, in order to have their aid in weaving the wall. After taking her hat, Columbine stands looking at the shepherds to see what is going on. They do not look at her. After a moment Thyrsis, slowly, with his eyes steadfastly on Corydon's, says, "Take it, and go." When Columbine comes in in the final scene, she is wearing the hat. She takes it off, however, as she sits down again at the table, so that the second beginning of the play may recall as vividly as possible to the audience the first beginning.

Edna St Vincent Millay – A Short Biography

Edna St. Vincent Millay was born on 22nd February 1892 in Rockland, Maine, the eldest of three daughters.

When she was 12, in 1904, her parents divorced. Although they had already been separated for some years her mother, Cora, had found life raising three daughters with its domestic abuse and the haphazard finances of a relationship with their father, Henry, too difficult. The four of them now moved from town to town, enduring various illnesses and living in poverty. Despite their circumstances their mother insisted on travelling with a trunk full of classic literature. Their one indulgence was to be able to read Shakespeare, Milton and other literary greats.

Edna did manage to keep up a remote relationship with her father thorough letters they sent each other for several years.

She loved the outdoors. One of her prime sources for poetic inspiration was Nature with its seasons of life and death, growth and decay. She would spend hours alone immersed in its company throughout her life.

After some time Cora and her daughters settled in a small house at the property of Cora's aunt in Camden, Maine. Finally with a semblance stability around her Edna began to write poetry. Her literary journey had begun.

All of the sisters were independently minded, speaking frankly and rubbing up against authority. Edna had decided she wished to be known as 'Vincent'. Her school principal in a display of petty authority called her by any other name that started with a 'V'.

Edna developed her literary talents at a furious rate. She began by being published in the Camden High School literary magazine, The Megunticook. At 14 she won the St. Nicholas Gold Badge for poetry, and by 15, she had published her poetry in the popular children's magazine St. Nicholas, the Camden Herald, and the high-profile anthology Current Literature.

In 1912, at the age of 20, she entered her poem 'Renascence' in The Lyric Year poetry contest. Despite being considered the best poem it was only given fourth place. The ensuing uproar brought Edna a lot of publicity. The winner, Orrick Johns, stated that 'Renascence' was the best poem, and that the 'award was as much an embarrassment to me as a triumph.' Another prize winner offered her his $250 prize money. In its aftermath the wealthy arts patron Caroline B. Dow heard Edna reciting her poetry and playing piano at the Whitehall Inn in Camden, Maine, and was so impressed that she offered to pay for her education at Vassar College.

By 1913, somewhat later than would be usual (she was 21) she entered Vassar College. She was not fully prepared for its strict regimen. The college expected its students to be refined and live according to their status as young women. Edna by now enjoyed the more liberal social aspects of life including drinking, smoking and flirting. She managed to combine both, continuing to write verse and also several plays.

She liberally engaged in relationships including several with women. She was keen to explore and experience more of life.

This experience included trenchant views on society and how it saw and valued women. During the years of the Great War Edna was an ardent pacifist, but her views on war would later change in a very dramatic fashion.

Edna graduated in 1917 and left for New York. Her life here was openly bisexual. Edna described her life as 'very, very poor and very, very merry.' This was evidently enhanced by her own natural beauty and frivolous nature, although these were only a mask to a more serious woman who was writing powerful poetry.

To provide income she worked with the Provincetown Players on Macdougal Street and the Theatre Guild.

Edna began to use her poetry, as she became more deeply engaged in feminist activism, to explore those themes. She soon had no hesitation in writing on subjects others found taboo.

She also had a remarkable way of gathering relationships and keeping her partners intensely loyal to her, even after, in the case of two suitors who happened to be literary critics, rejecting their marriage proposals.

Her ability to fall in and out of love together with the sometimes cold and raw New York environment seemed to move her poetry into shorter, pithier poems which were published in many magazines including Vanity Fair and the Forum

In 1919, she wrote the anti-war play 'Aria da Capo', which starred her sister Norma Millay and which played at the Provincetown Playhouse in New York City.

The following year, 1920, Edna published 'A Few Figs From Thistles'. Its subject matter of female sexuality and feminism was immediately criticized by many. But her reputation was only growing.

In January 1921 Europe beckoned and Edna went to Paris, where she met and befriended the sculptors Thelma Wood and Constantin Brancusi, the photographer Man Ray, and had various affairs. She also became pregnant. Although a marriage license was obtained Edna instead returned to New England where her mother helped induce an abortion with alkanet, as recommended in her old copy of 'Culpeper's Complete Herbal'.

Edna achieved significant fame when she won the Pulitzer Prize for Poetry in 1923 for 'The Ballad of the Harp-Weaver'. It was a magnificent triumph. She was also the third woman in six years to win this very prestigious award, following in the footsteps of Sara Teasdale (1918) and Margaret Widdemer (1919).

At a house party in Croton-on-Hudson, New York she met Eugen Jan Boissevain, a Dutch-born coffee importer. He was the widower of the labor lawyer and war correspondent Inez Milholland, a political icon Edna had met during her Vassar years.

On their wedding day a few months later, Edna fell ill with intestinal problems. Eugen drove her to Manhattan for emergency surgery. Edna, referring to her Pulitzer Prize, quipped, 'If I die now, at least I'll be immortal.' He nursed her back to health with remarkable devotion. He was a self-proclaimed feminist and encouraged her to write whilst he took care of everything else. Their marriage was open, and both took several lovers during its course.

In 1924 along with several others she helped to found the Cherry Lane Theater and its remit of staging experimental drama.

A further source of revenue was from short stories she wrote for the mass-market magazine Ainslee's. With these she stayed under the radar. To protect her poetic identity with its smaller and more serious audience, she used a pseudonym; Nancy Boyd. The publisher eventually offered to double her fees if he could use her real name. She refused.

In 1925, for $9000 they purchased 345 acres of farm and outbuildings called Steepletop near Austerlitz, New York, which had once been a blueberry farm, and then added another 300 acres. From a Sears Roebuck catalog kit they built a barn, and followed this with a writing cabin and a tennis court. Edna even found the time to grow her own vegetables.

Several years later they purchased Ragged Island in Casco Bay, Maine, as a summer retreat. Edna frequently had problems with the servants they employed and despite her liberal tendencies and social inclusiveness wrote 'The only people I really hate are servants. They are not really human beings at all.'

In the summer of 1936, Edna was riding in a station wagon when the door suddenly swung open. She was hurled into the pitch-darkness and rolled into a rock-strewn gully. She survived but with severely damaged nerves in her spine which required frequent surgeries and hospitalizations and at least daily doses of morphine. Edna was to live the rest of her life in pain.

By 1940 she was sufficiently alarmed by the rise of fascism to advocate for the U.S. to enter the war against the Axis powers. She later worked with the Writers' War Board and published a book of propaganda poems, 'Make Bright the Arrows: A 1940s Notebook', which managed to alienate even her most appreciative critics.

In 1942 in an article for The New York Times Magazine, Edna mourned the callous destruction of the Czechoslovak town of Lidice. Nazi forces had razed it to the ground, slaughtered its male inhabitants and scattered its surviving residents in retaliation for the assassination of Reinhard Heydrich. The article would serve as the basis of her 32-page poem, 'Murder of Lidice' in 1942.

In 1943, Edna was the sixth person and the second woman to be awarded the Frost Medal for her lifetime contribution to American poetry.

Despite the excellent sales of her books in the 1930s, her declining reputation, constant medical bills, and increasingly frequent demands from her mentally-ill sister Kathleen, meant that for most of her last years Edna was in debt to her publisher.

She did however quietly purchase a racing stable to indulge her passion for thoroughbred horse-racing. It would absorb much of her remaining income.

In 1949 after a twenty-six year marriage Boissevain died after a battle with lung cancer. Edna lived alone for the last year of her life. She drank heavily and lived almost as a recluse.

Edna St. Vincent Millay, after suffering a heart attack, fell down the stairs and died at her home on 19th October 1950. She was found approximately eight hours after her death. She was 58 years old.

She is buried alongside her husband at Steepletop, Austerlitz, New York.

Edna St Vincent Millay – A Concise Bibliography

Poems

Renascence & Other Poems (1917)
A Few Figs From Thistles: Poems & Four Sonnets (1920)
Second April (1921)
The Ballad of the Harp-Weaver (1922)
Poems (1923)
Distressing Dialogues, preface by Edna St. Vincent Millay (written as pseudonym Nancy Boyd) (1924)
The Buck in the Snow & Other Poems (1928)
Fatal Interview (Sonnets) (1931)
Wine from These Grapes (1934)
Conversation at Midnight (Narrative poem) (1937)
Huntsman, What Quarry? (1939)
There Are No Islands, Any More: Lines Written in Passion and in Deep Concern for England, France, and My Own Country (1940)
Make Bright the Arrows: 1940 Notebook (Poems) (1940)
The Murder of Lidice (Poem) (1942)
Second April and The Buck in the Snow, introduction by William Rose Benét (1950)
Mine the Harvest (Poems) (Edited by Norma Millay) (1954)

Translator

Flowers of Evil by Charles Baudelaire (with George Dillon) (1936)

Plays

Aria da capo (one-act play in verse; first produced in Greenwich Village, NY, December 5, 1919) (Also directed) (1921)
The Lamp and the Bell (Five-act play; first produced June 18, 1921)
Two Slatterns and a King: A Moral Interlude (1921)
Three Plays (Two Slatterns and a King, Aria da Capo, and The Lamp and the Bell) (1926)
The Princess Marries the Page (one-act play) (1932)

Opera

The King's Henchman (three-act play; New York, February 17, 1927) (Librettist)

Letters

Letters of Edna St. Vincent Millay (Edited by Allan Ross Macdougall) (1952)

www.ingramcontent.com/pod-product-compliance
Lightning Source LLC
Chambersburg PA
CBHW021949040426
42448CB00008B/1313